Original title:
Through the House of Time

Copyright © 2025 Creative Arts Management OÜ
All rights reserved.

Author: Aurora Sinclair
ISBN HARDBACK: 978-1-80587-226-9
ISBN PAPERBACK: 978-1-80587-696-0

The Diary of Time's Embrace

Tick-tock, the clock does dance,
As I trip on fate's own pants.
Pages flip, oh what a tease,
Forgotten snacks beneath the squeeze.

Yesterday's socks in pairs untold,
Echoes of stories that once were bold.
Laughter spills from dusty halls,
As my toaster threatens to take my falls.

Silhouettes in the Twilight

Shadows prance across the wall,
A lizard leaps, do we call?
Twilight giggles with a grin,
Guess who just forgot to bin!

Dinner plates in heavy stacks,
Voices rise, we crack some jokes.
Chasing echoes in the night,
As my cat plots a silly fright.

Memorable Corners of a Faded Home

A chair that squeaks with every sigh,
Whispers of years whisper by.
Old puzzles missing all their parts,
Promises lost on leapfrog carts.

Each corner holds a secret caper,
Balloons that never left the paper.
Shoeprints lead to nowhere grand,
As we dance, a three-legged band.

The Seasons of a Crumbling Roof

Raindrops play on tin can drums,
We shuffle 'round, escape the hums.
Eavesdropping on a squirrel's tale,
While my umbrella tries to bail.

Winter whispers with a snowy sneeze,
Then summer's sun has cats at ease.
Each season shares a funny tune,
Beneath this wobbly, bandaged moon.

Tokens of Temporal Tenderness

When clocks giggle, they tick-tock,
Even a cat wore a wristwatch!
Potatoes dance in the kitchen light,
As socks argue in a playful fight.

A spoon tried to stir up some fun,
As forks played tag, oh what a run!
Dishes laughed beneath moon's glow,
While dust bunnies put on a show.

The calendar winked, marked a day,
Where yesterday's clothes slid out to play.
Pants with stripes tell tales so tall,
Of when they tripped and had a fall.

In moments captured, laughter swells,
As time plays tricks with silly spells.
Each tick a giggle, each tock a sigh,
In this grand jest where seconds fly.

Shadows of Forgotten Lullabies

In corners hidden, whispers creep,
As shadows gather, secrets keep.
A teddy bear sings off-key,
While pillows laugh in harmony.

The night cap giggles under the moon,
While lampshades sway to a funny tune.
Worn-out slippers shuffle and slide,
As bedtime stories come alive and hide.

The clock does a jig, one-two-three,
As dust motes whirl in pure glee.
Old shoes reminisce of steps they've taken,
In dreams of laughter, never forsaken.

Lullabies buried beneath the floor,
Open the door to tales of yore.
In this shadowy dance of night,
All is forgotten, but joy takes flight.

The Glistening of Time's Remnants

A shiny spoon from yesteryears,
Hums a tune to chase away fears.
Cookies crumble from time's embrace,
As crumbs form a silly race.

The wallpaper grins, patterns askew,
Telling tales of things we once knew.
An old clock struts like a proud knight,
Tickling seconds with all its might.

A phantom mop sweeps up the past,
Waltzing through time's endless cast.
Forgotten hats dance in delight,
In the quirkiness of candlelight.

Each glimmer tells of laughter lost,
In the chaos of days and the cost.
Through remnants that sparkle and shine,
We find hilarity in the design.

Bridges of Memory

Old photos giggle from shelves so high,
At fashions that made past eras fly.
Grandpa's mustache twirls with flair,
While grandma's heels lead a waltzing air.

Paper hearts flutter, secrets in fold,
In every corner, a story is told.
A dust cloud forms a giggling crew,
As memories leap like a spry kangaroo.

An echo of laughter from days gone by,
Sails through windows, waving goodbye.
As kids in the yard, all silly and wild,
Remind us to play like a carefree child.

Bridges of memory, strong and bright,
Link us to joy in the soft twilight.
With every step on this fleeting ground,
A dance of happiness can be found.

Vaults of Yesterday's Dreams

In the attic of lost socks,
Lies a pirate's wooden leg.
The cat claims it for her throne,
While I sip on cold eggnog.

A clock that ticks in reverse,
Tells tales of lunch at dawn.
My sandwich went out to roam,
To see if it could spawn.

Old photos laugh at my hair,
Each frizz a story told.
I'll never trust a mullet,
It promised me pure gold.

Through the vaults, I trip and slide,
On marbles once held dear.
Each step replays the past,
And whispers, "Have a beer!"

The Stillness Between Heartbeats

In the silence of my chest,
The cat plots a grand heist.
She swipes my half-eaten toast,
Turns out, that was her advice.

Wait, did I just hear a joke?
Or was that just my brain?
It's hard to tell in still air,
If silence hides the insane.

The clock chuckles where it hangs,
As if it knows the punchline.
I ponder if I'm a fool,
Autocorrect says I'm divine.

Yet, in this paused moment's breath,
A giggle breaks the calm.
Every heartbeat's spare humor,
Is a tickle in the psalm.

Beneath the Timeless Veil

Behind the curtain hangs a shoe,
From a dance I never had.
It sways and spins with glee,
While I sit, utterly sad.

Under the veil, I see bright lights,
A disco ball's dizzy gleam.
But my socks are mismatched now,
Seems fate's lost its own theme.

The roast in the oven's gone wild,
Told it to bake for a minute.
Now it's a charred opera,
Singing 'Why'd you begin it?'

This timeless place ticks away,
With laughter of long-lost cheer.
Every giggle echoes here,
And I dance with my fear.

Grapevines of Memory's Whisper

In the garden, time's a vine,
Twisting tales of days gone past.
My childhood hides among the leaves,
Laughs at how long it can last.

The sunflowers recall my dreams,
Of becoming a brave knight.
But swords turned to butter knives,
All those battles lost their fight.

Each grape plucked holds a story,
About jam left on toast.
The pantry's the brawl arena,
For crumbs I now love most.

Whispers linger, soft and sweet,
From memories drifting by.
With each chuckle, life replays,
In the garden; oh my, oh my!

Tales Etched in Shadows

In corners where dust bunnies reign,
Old socks hold court, there's laughter to gain.
The cat's nap kingdom, a furry delight,
While clocks tick-tock, turning day into night.

A fridge full of leftovers, all past their prime,
With each door's creak, we dance out of time.
The portraits on walls seem to wink at me,
As I trip over shoes that just won't agree.

The echo of footsteps from ages gone by,
Whispers of mischief that fly through the sky.
Each mirror reflects a strangely dressed ghost,
Who waves with a grin, like he's ready to toast.

With puzzles and riddles in each little nook,
I find treasure maps hidden in every book.
So here's to the moments, absurd and sublime,
In this merry chaos, I laugh at the rhyme.

The Lanterns of Memory's Passage

A light flickers softly, with tales of the past,
While mismatched socks argue, as friendships are cast.
The hallways waltz with shadows so bold,
Spinning stories of laughter that never grow old.

The cupboard hums softly, with cookies long gone,
What did we bake? Oh! The smell lingers on.
In the garden, gnomes grin, their secrets in tow,
Like they're gossiping wildly, as the winds of time blow.

A chair that creaks gently, tells me the news,
Of family gatherings and old, silly views.
With glasses all empty and stories half spun,
We gather at dusk, for the giggles and fun.

And there on the mantel, a trophy of cheer,
For the one who can tell the best joke of the year,
So let's raise our lanterns, let memories swirl,
In this house of laughter, we'll dance and we'll twirl.

Residue of Ancient Laughs

Ghosts of giggles roam the halls,
Tickling dust on ancient walls.
A jester's hat on a shelf so high,
Whispers of jokes that never die.

A cat in a wig, oh what a sight,
Chasing shadows in the pale moonlight.
Grandma's slippers dance with glee,
As we share her tales over tea.

Socks mismatched, a fashion faux pas,
The toaster burps, what a bizarre.
Nostalgia's laughter spills like wine,
Every corner holds a punchline.

Old clocks chuckle, their hands go round,
Tickling time without a sound.
In this space of memory's play,
Ancient laughs forever stay.

A Symphony of Tick-Tock

Tick-tock chimed the old grandfather,
Dancing shadows, oh what a lather!
With every tick, a funny dance,
A rhythm that sparked the oddest romance.

The cuckoo sang in quarrelsome tones,
While rats in capes made for funny drones.
Time-worn rhythms, a hapless feat,
With metronomes tapping their silly feet.

Watch out for clocks with naughty schemes,
As seconds sneak into our dreams.
In a race where time is a prankster's muse,
Every tick brings laughter we can't refuse.

So gather 'round, in this grand time play,
With giggles and chuckles, we pass the day.
A symphony where seconds misalign,
Silly and sweet, this dance divine.

Suns of Lost Horizons

Sunrise giggles peek through the pane,
As sleepy heads shake off the rain.
Yesterday's socks tell tales so odd,
While birds in sunglasses applaud.

Each horizon hides a silly surprise,
A chicken in shoes that never ties.
Rainbow wonders in laughter's embrace,
Chasing the suns at a comical pace.

In puddles, reflections of shapes divine,
Jumping right in, we toe the line.
Finding joy in a shadow's quick prank,
Like whispers of wishing wells by the bank.

So let's take a ride on this merry-go-round,
Where time skip and spills laughter abound.
With suns that giggle at skies of blue,
Making memories in a playful hue.

The Mirror of Time's Passage

In the hall of mirrors, reflections tease,
Silly faces in a comical breeze.
A laugh from the past makes an entrance loud,
Dwarfed by the mirror, lost in the crowd.

Faded dreams in eccentric frames,
Dancing shadows, playing games.
Mirrors chuckle, their gleam so bright,
Time's mishaps caught in the soft moonlight.

Yet every wrinkle tells a joke,
As laughter swirls in a happy cloak.
In the dance of days, they tease and sing,
With every glance, a giggle takes wing.

Thus in this hall, where time stands still,
We find the laughter and the thrill.
In reflections of joy that never fade,
The mirror smiles, and we serenade.

Leaves of Autumn's Embrace

Leaves tumble down in a dizzying dance,
Squirrels debate on which nut's the best chance.
Pumpkins sit grinning, their faces quite round,
While ghosts in the garden play tag on the ground.

Sweaters come out, all itchy and bright,
Hot cider in hand, we're drinking with delight.
The crunch of the leaves makes us laugh out loud,
As the wind joins in, blowing leaves like a crowd.

Kids trick-or-treating in costumes so wild,
A dragon meets a ghost; oh, what fun we've compiled!
With laughter and snacks, the hours just fly,
As autumn's embrace drifts like clouds in the sky.

Attunements in the Dust

A clock ticks loudly, yet time seems to freeze,
Dust bunnies dance as they float with such ease.
Books stacked up high, a real tower of fun,
Each page a story, the adventures begun.

Wipe off the shelves with a playful flick,
Surprises are hiding, it's a neat little trick!
Old toys peek out from their colorful tombs,
Inviting us back to our childhood rooms.

Laughter erupts from a long-lost cassette,
A song that we loved, and we still can't forget.
We hum and we sway, lost in the dust,
Attuning our hearts, in the past we trust.

Vignettes of a Faded Era

In sepia tones, the old photos laugh,
A curious cat took a curious bath.
A hat on a hatstand, so proud and so tall,
Next to it stands a mustard-stained wall.

Grandpa with stories that tickle the ear,
A story of a time when things were quite queer.
He swings his long cane and mimics a dance,
As grandma rolls eyes and gives him a glance.

Old records spin with a delightful crack,
We join in the chorus, and never look back.
Each vignette glimmers, a chuckle in frame,
All wrapped up in laughter, they're never the same.

The Gallery of Fleeting Wink

In the gallery where memories hang,
Each smile a snapshot, and each laugh is a clang.
A wink from the past, like a jest from a friend,
Reminds us of moments that never quite end.

Twirling umbrellas with glee in the rain,
A whoopee cushion; oh, the delightful pain!
Time flits about in a quirky parade,
As we chase after giggles that never quite fade.

Each photo a portal, we jump in with glee,
Dancing with shadows who were young and quite free.
In this gallery timeless, where joy has a twink,
Snapshots of laughter are what we all think.

Threads of Nostalgia

Old photos hang with silly grins,
Each snapshot whispers tales of sins.
We dance through halls of goofy grace,
Forgotten styles, a wild embrace.

The cat in hats from days gone wrong,
Mismatched socks, a fashion strong.
Tiny shoes that surely squeak,
In laughter's echo, memories peak.

Grandma's feasts and tales so tall,
How Auntie fell, like leaves in fall.
Time tickles us, we laugh and twirl,
At every memory, life's a whirl.

Intervals of Reflection

In the attic lies a rocking chair,
Where wobbly dreams float through the air.
Dusty dolls with creepy smiles,
Remind us of our younger trials.

We sip on tea with spoons a-clink,
While pondering why socks disappear in the sink.
Time hops like a frog, so absurd,
A jumble of moments, all blurred.

Tick-tock goes the clock, quite mad,
Reminds us of joys and things we had.
We search for treasures wrapped in yarn,
Only to find a relic of a barn.

Celestial Murmurs of Olden Days

Stars twinkle like sequins on a dress,
Whispers of yore make us confess.
Uncle Bob's tales take flight,
Of aliens dancing in the night.

Granddad's stories, both strange and bright,
Involve a rabbit who took to flight.
Time winks at us with its cheeky play,
As we chuckle at the past's display.

The sun did rise, the moon did sway,
While we fumbled through our clumsy ballet.
Each tickle of time, a playful tease,
Reminding us to laugh with ease.

The Ancestral Gallery

A portrait stares with mismatched eyes,
What secrets hide beneath those lies?
Grandma's bun in a beehive style,
Makes us giggle, oh what a while!

The family tree spreads wide and tall,
Branches chuckle, and leaves enthrall.
Each ancestor, a ghostly friend,
Who'd surely giggle at the trends.

We shuffle through this time-worn hall,
Where echoes bounce, on the walls they call.
In every picture, a jesting glance,
As we spin our tales in this lively dance.

Among Echoes and Etchings

In dusty corners, laughter reigns,
Old toys giggle, dancing in chains.
Paintings whisper, secrets to share,
Footnotes of life linger in air.

Shadows flicker, playful and spry,
Socks have stories that leap and fly.
The clock is ticklish, it tells a joke,
As time swirls in a merry cloak.

Footprints in Twilight

Footprints tiptoe on the floor,
Each step a giggle, wanting more.
Echoes bumble into the night,
Chasing shadows, oh what a sight!

Stairs creak softly, a cheeky tune,
Whispers of mischief under the moon.
A hat on the cat, what a sight to see,
Time spins sideways, wild and free.

The Library of Lives Lived

Books stack up like wobbly towers,
Pages flapping like playful flowers.
Characters waltz from spine to spine,
Laughing at plots, oh-so-divine!

Ink spills tales of silly strife,
Where lampshades dream of a different life.
Bookmarks giggle, peeking out bright,
In this library, all is light.

Recollections in the Gloom

Cobbwebs chuckle across the room,
While ghosts in pajamas play with the gloom.
A rogue chair dances on squeaky wheels,
Whispering of tomfoolery, what a deal!

In corners, memories drop like coins,
Creating music from forgotten joints.
Ticking clocks snicker at time's own game,
As laughter echoes, never the same.

Whispers of Yesterday

Old socks dance with glee,
As chairs gossip near the tree.
Dust bunnies hold court with pride,
While photo frames quietly chide.

Grandpa's tales make cats roll eyes,
As time flies by in funny lies.
The clock ticks loud, yet sleeps so deep,
In corners where the giggles creep.

In the Hallways of Hours

In corridors where echoes play,
Socks leap out with things to say.
Tick-tock mats with silly flair,
Dance in rhythm, unaware.

Each door swings wide to spill bright cheer,
Where memories laugh, with no one near.
Walls hum with stories yet untold,
In a tune that never gets old.

Gateways to Distant Yesterdays

A wardrobe creaks, a goblin sneers,
As time slips by in fits of cheers.
Past's popcorn pops in every nook,
Where old toys plot and stew and cook.

The pantry holds a dance or two,
With pickles that just want to woo.
Each cupboard opens with a grin,
As shadows wiggle, let the fun begin!

The Attic of Lost Dreams

In the attic's cozy lap,
Old dreams sit and take a nap.
Bicycles rust in mid-laugh flight,
While dolls plot mischief every night.

A trunk holds secrets dressed in fun,
Whispering tales of races run.
The dust motes twirl, they take a bow,
As clowns juggle time, here and now.

Windows to Fading Days

Dusty panes and half-sketched dreams,
Cats wear monocles, or so it seems.
The clock's a prankster, ticks back and forth,
Chasing an hour that ran out of worth.

Time sips tea with a crooked grin,
Baking muffins with absent-minded kin.
Sunbeams stumble through curtains of lace,
Winking at memories, keeping their space.

Portraits of the Unseen Past

Frames collapse in laughter's glee,
Grandpa's wig makes a fine mockery.
A cousin's ghost tries to take a bow,
But trips on the rug, oh, what a row!

A lady in a bonnet, quite the fuss,
Whispers to walls, 'Don't make a fuss!'
Each brushstroke alive with tales untold,
All while the artist sneezed out a mold.

Footsteps on the Timeworn Floor

Squeaky pauses in the silent night,
Shadows shimmy, what a funny sight!
Footprints boogie, a dance long past,
In a dwelling where time has amassed.

Stumbling echoes of old chitchat,
Mice giggle, 'Did you hear that?'
A creaky board tells tales galore,
While dust bunnies roll, demanding encore.

Lanterns of Unwritten Stories

Flickering lights with stories to tell,
Each wiggle of flame rings a silly bell.
A mouse with a hat gives a cheeky nod,
To secrets kept close by the family odd.

Jars filled with whispers, giggles contained,
Dreams of a cat who once ruled unchained.
The lanterns blink, their tales they share,
In a world where laughter floats in the air.

Shadows of Ages Forgotten

In corners where whispers reside,
Old socks and laughter collide.
The cat naps on history's lap,
While mice theorize in a cheese trap.

Grandpa's tall tales grow taller still,
As cookies make the hippos thrill.
The clock giggles, it's running slow,
While time plays hopscotch with a crow.

Dust bunnies play hide and seek,
As calendars blush, all rosy and meek.
The walls hold secrets, sipping tea,
While shadows dance quite merrily.

Forgotten ages stumble about,
In slippers of silence, they dance and pout.
Tick-tock, the thrills of yesteryear,
Every hour holds a fit of cheer.

A Tapestry of Seconds

Stitch by stitch, the moments blend,
A hiccup, a laugh, around the bend.
Bobbleheads cheer, the clock sways,
In a tapestry of wild, silly ways.

In the kitchen, pasta sings,
As onions jump with funky flings.
A spoon of time, a ladle of fun,
In this quilt, oh so well spun!

Each second, a patch, a quirky spree,
Like socks abandoned, lost at sea.
Bright colors dance, mischief in thread,
As ticklish tales of noodles are spread.

With every laugh, a stitch we weave,
In moments so punchy, we can't believe.
A fabric of seconds, so absurd,
In this house, every whim's preferred.

Windows to Eternity

Peeking through panes of peculiar sights,
With giggles and grins, not typical nights.
The moon winks at the lazy sun,
In a cosmic game of tag, such fun!

Rainbows tumble; the clouds chat away,
As chickens plan a grand ballet.
The wind writes poems in the trees,
While squirrels debate the best of cheese.

Windows open to tales untold,
Of pancake pilots who dream of gold.
A new dawn whispers, "Let's pray to the toast!"
As memories toast to the future they boast.

Through frames that frame the absurd spectacle,
Laughter echoes, oh what a spectacle!
Eternity giggles; it's quite the spree,
With windows wide to absurdity.

The Dust of Days Gone By

In a shoebox where time loves to hide,
Old fortunes and trinkets, side by side.
The dust mites dance to a retro beat,
As mischief bubbles underneath their feet.

Hats from the past, with silly flair,
Mingle with memories, unaware.
They tip their brims, then start to jive,
The parties of yore, they come alive!

Each speck of dust spins a tale,
Of ice cream dreams and a goofy snail.
While grandmas shuffle with a wink,
A ruckus in the attic, don't you think?

Days gone by giggle and sway,
With a twist of fate in a playful display.
The specks of life, in sunshine's sigh,
The dust of days forever nigh.

The Echoing Silence of Yesterdays

In the attic, dust bunnies play,
Old toys giggle at yesterday.
The clock ticks backwards, oh what a sight,
As cats wear hats, so silly, so bright.

Downstairs, the fridge hums a tune,
Leftovers dance under the moon.
Grandpa cracks jokes about his old bike,
While socks throw shade, yikes, all alike.

Laughter echoes through shadows so thin,
As old curtains whisper, "Let's begin!"
Each creak of the floor, a comic refrain,
Joy lives here, wrapped in the mundane.

So raise a glass to those silly days,
Where laughter echoes through baffling ways.
For time may jog, trip, or even slip,
But joy in the past? That's quite the trip!

Timeless Reflections

Mirrors giggle, showing old styles,
With hairdos gone rogue, and vintage smiles.
The past winks back, a mischievous ghost,
In pajamas from ages past, we toast.

Sunbeams flicker with stories untold,
Full of jests, and a few brave and bold.
The worn-out chair squeaks, 'Take a seat!'
While carpets roll back in retreat.

Cooking up chaos in the kitchen, oh dear,
Pasta on walls, the sauce, 'disappears'.
While dishes complain, "What a mess!"
With smiles of humor, we'll just confess.

Time travels forward, yet stands still,
In corners with echoes, we laugh, we thrill.
So here's to reflections, both funny and true,
In a world where nothing is ever quite new.

Rooms of Fleeting Dreams

Rooms filled with laughter, echoing bright,
Where pillows collide in a playful fight.
The walls growing ears to the whispers we share,
While night lights dance in their dreamy affair.

In the closet, a monster hums a tune,
While dust mites juggle beneath the moon.
Socks go dancing when we're not around,
Creating a mess, oh what joy they've found!

Chairs are slumping, they've had enough fun,
Claiming their space, "We need to run!"
Yet stories are painted in every nook,
Where laughter and chaos are the main hook.

So let's embrace these fleeting delights,
In rooms where the imagination ignites.
For dreams are the ticket to laughter's parade,
Where memories shimmer and never quite fade.

Fragmented Memories

Pieces of laughter scattered about,
In corners where shadows wiggle and shout.
The crumbs of the past are a tasty refrain,
Cooking up chaos from stains on the pane.

Old photo albums tumble and slide,
Where smiles get goofy, the laughter won't hide.
With stories that twist like a playful cat,
Of socks on the ceiling and a dog on a mat.

In the drawer, mismatched memories reside,
Where spoons wear hats, emotions collide.
Tick-tock on the wall, what a quirky chime,
Whispering giggles of a wobbly time.

So gather the pieces, let's craft a new tale,
Of silly adventures that never grow stale.
In fragmented memories, let's whine with glee,
For the joy of the past is still bold and free!

Unraveling the Threads of Time

Once I found a sock, oh dear,
Its match was lost, so it did leer.
A time-traveling pair, they say,
But one got stuck on laundry day.

My grandma swears she met a bear,
Who danced and twirled without a care.
She dropped her tea and fled outside,
While Grandpa laughed, his laugh a tide.

A clock strikes two, and then it grins,
It flips through seconds like old sins.
Each tick a joke, each tock a pun,
In this weird world, we're all just fun.

Last week I tried to bake a pie,
But all my apples chose to fly.
They zoomed through time in search of zest,
Left me with a curious mess.

Vignettes of an Endless Cycle

In gardens where the daisies spin,
I paused to watch a beetle grin.
It rolled a ball made of pure dirt,
Declaring 'I'm the king of hurt!'

The toaster popped, my bread took flight,
It soared and danced, a lovely sight.
With butter on its wings, it flew,
A breakfast dream, my heart it wooed.

The cat, aghast, watched every move,
As time was bending, caught in groove.
It stared and plotted, then took aim,
To pounce on moments just the same.

A squirrel's tale, a chef's delight,
Creating chaos, pure and bright.
In loops and swirls, it twirls away,
Forever caught in this ballet.

Echoes of Moments Past

I heard the fridge hum songs of yore,
Each note a snack I can't ignore.
The leftovers dance, all dressed in green,
A party where no one's ever seen.

The calendar tries to run away,
With every month it starts to sway.
'Catch me if you can!' it shouts with glee,
As I chase it 'round, one-two and three.

A funny hat upon my head,
Reflects the thoughts that I once said.
It whispers tales of days gone by,
And chuckles softly, 'Don't be shy!'

Each photo frame holds moments tight,
Where goofy faces bring pure delight.
They wink and nod, with time to pass,
These echoes leave a merry sass.

The Clock's Whisper

The clock's loud tick is quite a hoot,
It really loves to play the flute.
With every chime, a silly joke,
A laugh erupts, it's quite bespoke.

In the hallway, shoes run over,
In one hand, pizza, in the other, clover.
They laugh and shout, 'We own the night!'
Time taps its foot, it's quite the sight.

A wobbly chair begins to spin,
With every sway, a cheeky grin.
It creaks and sighs with every beat,
As time itself shuffles its feet.

So when the moon comes out to play,
Remember to dance the night away.
For moments are fleeting, silly, and bright,
Just like a clock that's lost in flight.

Shadows in the Attic

In the attic, dust bunnies play,
Whispering stories of yesterday.
Old toys giggle in a pile,
While shadows wear a cheeky smile.

A grandpa clock ticks away the gloom,
Counting laughs in a cluttered room.
Mice in hats, a tea party set,
Wondering if we'll join them yet.

Old hats joke about fashion trends,
While damp cardboard box breaks and bends.
Loud squeaks and giggles fill the space,
As we hold our breath for the next race.

A lost sock waves at the light,
As ghosts of memories take flight.
Come join us for a raucous cheer,
The attic's alive, let's persevere!

The Lullaby of Long-ago

Napping on a dusty shelf,
A clock sings softly to itself.
When did we last tick-tock in sync?
Time likes to giggle, don't you think?

Balloons float on air so light,
Reminding us of every bright night.
Lollipops and candy so grand,
Dance through dreams, hand-in-hand.

Photos blink like fast old films,
Promising laughter, and whims.
In the beanbag, a cat snores deep,
While echoes of joy happily creep.

We ride on memories, not alone,
Finding treasures in every zone.
Crib sheets wave to the skies so blue,
In our hearts, time still dances too.

The Forgotten Corners of Memory

In the corners where dust settles down,
Lies a smile from once upon a clown.
His laughter echoes soft yet loud,
In shadows where mischief is allowed.

Old shoes loiter with a daring grace,
Hoping to step into a new place.
With a wink and a hop, they dream,
Each scuff holds a silly scheme.

The rug whispers tales of a sock fight,
Carried forth in the dead of night.
The pet goldfish sports a silly grin,
While faded walls sing of where we've been.

In these corners, giggles reside,
Where time takes a playful ride.
With each frolic, we shall explore,
The treasures of laughter forevermore!

Dance of the Seasons Past

Springtime bags of potato chips,
Recounting tales of summer trips.
Leaves rustle with a tickled glee,
Waving at us, 'Come dance with me!'

Summer suns with made-up fronds,
Brought ice cream cones and funny bonds.
A loop of crows, in synchronized flight,
Cackling jokes till the last light.

Autumn's crunch sounds like a song,
With pumpkins in hats, all feeling strong.
Whirling leaves, a comical parade,
As memories of fun never fade.

Winter snickers, in frosty breath,
Chasing snowflakes to playful death.
With every twirl and jolly cheer,
Time's dance rolls on, year after year!

The Clockwork Heart

Tick tock, my heart does race,
As seconds dance, they leave no trace.
A winding key upon my chest,
Who knew that time could be so jest?

In every corner, clocks will chime,
They laugh and tease, oh what a crime!
With gears that squeak and springs that twang,
My heart's a tune, a merry clang!

A rabbit hops, a turtle glides,
Time's silly game, it never hides.
Each tick a joke, a ticklish beat,
I can't keep up, can't find my feet!

So here's to clocks and all their quirks,
Their playful ticks and silly jerks.
In every tick, a chuckle's found,
In this mad race, we all are bound.

Whispers from Another Era

In grand old halls where echoes dwell,
I hear the past with tales that swell.
A ghost with glasses sips his tea,
And tells me jokes from 1733!

Old paintings wink, their eyes a dance,
While chandeliers spin in a comical prance.
The portraits laugh and beckon near,
They say, "Join us, take a sip of cheer!"

A knight in armor cracks a grin,
"Time flies fast, so let's begin!"
With every tick, a tale is spun,
A far-off past, a joke run!

So let's toast to whispers from the past,
Where silly stories forever last.
With every laugh, we shatter gloom,
In this grand house, let laughter bloom!

A Journey Beyond the Sandglass

Once upon a grain so fine,
A trip that wasn't quite divine.
I tried to ride a falling sand,
But tripped and fell—oh, wasn't planned!

With each small grain that slipped away,
I lost my hat, that fickle sway.
The sands declared, "You're quite the clown!"
As I sat bothered, upside down!

A merry dance in a swirling storm,
Each granule's journey was quite the norm.
Laughter boomed, it filled the room,
As I tumbled through humorous doom!

But halting just to take a pause,
I found my joy beneath the flaws.
In every laugh and every fall,
A trip through time is best of all!

Memory's Labyrinth

In winding halls where echoes play,
I lose my socks, they stray away!
Dancing shoes on every shelf,
"Oh where's my hat?" I ask myself!

A maze of thoughts, a jumbled scheme,
Where every memory's just a dream.
I bump into a friendly face,
"Did we just meet? Or lose our place?"

My thoughts a whirl, a guessing game,
Each turn feels odd, yet still the same.
I chase my thoughts like pesky flies,
While laughter echoes with great surprise!

But in the end, what's lost is found,
In every laugh, joy knows no bound.
So let's embrace this puzzled art,
For in the chaos, lives the heart!

Echoes Beneath the Stairs

Whispers linger, can't escape,
A sock once lost, now takes shape.
Ghostly giggles from the past,
Chasing shadows, oh so fast.

In the kitchen, pots will clang,
As if to dance, they laugh and hang.
A spoon's a singer, oh what a show,
To kitchen chaos, the cacti grow.

Worn-out shoes trip on the floor,
Who knew they'd hold so much lore?
Every corner spins a tale,
Of mismatched socks that fade and pale.

Yet in this mess, a joy takes flight,
Each moment's silly, each moment's bright.
So let the echoes sing and play,
In this time-warped home, we'll sway.

The Tapestry of Fleeting Moments

Threads of laughter, colors blend,
A yarn of mishaps, no clear end.
Tangled stories, stitched with care,
Bright patchwork memories, we all share.

Frogs that leap from grandma's shoe,
Caught mid-flight, what else is new?
Mom's a juggler, pies on her head,
While Dad invents the dance of bread.

Ticking clocks that race ahead,
But who knew time could be so spread?
Chasing minutes like a game of tag,
With every hour, more laughs we brag.

So let's unravel this woven spree,
Moments silly, wild, and free.
In every loop, a ticklish cheer,
This tapestry we hold so dear.

Dust Motions in the Evening Light

Dust bunnies waltz across the floor,
In the golden glow, they crave some more.
A chair creaks, with wonders to tell,
As a light bulb winks, like it's under a spell.

Curtains flutter, secrets unfold,
As mismatched socks dare to be bold.
The cat blinks twice at a phantom sigh,
"What's all the fuss?" it seems to cry.

Old toys chuckle, they know the game,
Once cherished, now noble, yet still the same.
Every corner holds a playful tease,
Under fading light, how time likes to freeze.

So let the dust dance, oh what a sight,
In this magical, fleeting light.
We giggle at shadows and join the play,
For each evening has something to say.

Remnants of Joy in Silent Halls

Silent halls speak, a giggle or two,
Footsteps echo, who is it, boo?
A broom stands guard, with tales of dust,
In corners where all things rust.

Pictures grin with eyes so bright,
As time marches on in silly delight.
Whispers of cake on birthdays past,
Who forgot to count, oh what a blast!

Old slippers squeak, they beg for a dance,
While couches plot in a fabric romance.
Every creak tells a joke or two,
As memories tap-dance just for you.

In the silence, joy lingers near,
The sweetest echoes we hold dear.
Let's laugh with ghosts, in halls we roam,
In remnants of joy, we find our home.

Fragments of a Distant Echo

Once I heard a kitchen pot,
Singing to a wobbly cat.
It danced upon the tabletops,
Wishing it was more than that.

The clock tickled my ear near,
Chasing dust bunnies with cheer.
They giggled as they ran away,
Shouting, 'Catch us, if you dare!'

A shoe lay flat, a sock with glee,
Arguing who could disagree.
The walls whispered silly truths,
Of forgotten days and youthful spoofs.

In shadows deep, the laughter spun,
Reflecting on a time once fun.
Echoes of the night so bright,
In the house where jokes took flight.

The Canopy of What Was

Beneath the laughs of wooden beams,
A squirrel plotted silly schemes.
It stole my hat, ran up the wall,
Then slipped and gave a clumsy fall.

The lamp has tales of tangled wires,
Daydreams of electric fires.
It flickered, winked, then shone so bold,
As if to say, 'I'm tired of old!'

In corners dark, the spiders prance,
Holding an annual dance of chance.
With tiny hats and shoes so neat,
They twirled in rhythm—had two left feet!

Amidst the dust, the memories swirl,
Of playful days and every twirl.
A tapestry of laughter bright,
Under the canopy of light.

A Stroll Through Faded Halls

As I tiptoe through the hallway,
Every creak leads me astray.
A ghost in slippers winks at me,
Saying, 'Join our jamboree!'

Framed portraits with a cheeky grin,
Whisper ludes, 'You're late again!'
There's a dance of shadows at play,
Making fun of yesterday.

An old vacuum lost its charm,
Claiming dust was there to harm.
But every tumble just won't do,
It swears it's smarter than a shoe!

And so I stroll, a comic show,
With laugh tracks echoing low.
In faded halls where stories bloom,
Residing ghostly nuts in a room.

The Legacy of Dusty Footfalls

Through crannies deep, the footfalls plod,
Telling tales that seem quite odd.
With every step, they chance to trip,
Leaving giggles on our trip.

A mopping bucket bounced in mirth,
Claiming every drop its worth.
But slippery floors don't care for pride,
As I take a funny slide.

The fridge hums tunes from long ago,
Whispers of leftovers in tow.
It judges each snack with a sigh,
'Oh, broccoli, why'd you say goodbye?'

Yet here I stand, a time-warped fool,
In this whirlwind of playful rule.
The legacy of laughter calls,
In my home of dusty footfalls.

Archive of Vanished Days

In corners where the dust bunnies play,
Faded photos laugh at the bright decay.
Yesterday's laundry still wriggles about,
Socks from matches that lived without doubt.

Old clocks snicker, hands spinning away,
Tick-tock dances in a comical fray.
Cupcakes chased elves in absurd little dreams,
All the while scheming to steal all the creams.

A cat with a monocle sits with its grin,
Plotting a caper while wagging its chin.
Dishes conspire, refusing to dry,
Winking in silence, "We'll never comply!"

So flip through these pages, with laughter abide,
For vanished days hold the silliest ride.
Every memory wiggles with whimsical flair,
In this archive of nonsense, come breathe in the air.

Perpetual Threading

A needle once danced with a yarn ball round,
Stitching odd patterns no one had found.
Quilts of mishaps, folks giggling with glee,
Warped by the tales of a delightful spree.

Grandma's odd sweaters, all tangled and bright,
Chased by the dog in a footrace of fright.
Purls turning plays into fiber-filled fun,
Knots in the fabric, oh how they have spun!

Laces of laughter weave stories so grand,
Each loopful a moment of whimsy unplanned.
Each stitch tells a tale that tickles the mind,
Not one of them serious, all of them blind.

So thread on through life, with mischief and cheer,
For in every seam lies a joke to endear.
Whether tangled or woven, delightfully frayed,
A perpetual threading by giggles displayed.

The Haunting of Old Spaces

There's a ghost in the attic, a prankster at best,
Who rearranges the books with a laugh and a jest.
Chairs rattle in rhythm, a dance just for fun,
While old doors creak sideways—who says ghosts can't run?

The kitchen is bubbling with pots that can't wait,
Casseroles jump at the prospect of fate.
Spices giggle softly, confused by the time,
As walls are embraced in a waltz so sublime.

Basements are filled with forgotten delight,
Where treasures live on in the glow of moonlight.
Each corner a joke wrapped in cobwebs and dust,
The echoes of laughter inspire a robust.

So whisper your secrets, let silliness soar,
For the haunting of spaces is never a bore.
With each little chuckle, old memories play,
In corners and shadows, the fun finds its way.

The Memory Ledger

Flip through the pages of the ledger of laughs,
Where funny mistakes are the best kind of gaffs.
On page twenty-seven, a cake fell askew,
While cats in tuxedos baked muffins for two.

There's a doodle of Grandpa, a mustache so grand,
Attempting to juggle with jelly in hand.
A note says, "The trampoline? No, not today!"
When Uncle Lou soared and then flew far away.

Pages turn yellow yet still shimmer bright,
With tales of wild dances late into the night.
Each line a chuckle, each scribble a spree,
In this ledger of memories, joyous and free.

So pen down the laughter, the mishaps, the glee,
For each little moment is splendid, you see.
Turn back the clock just to giggle once more,
In the memory ledger, life happens galore.

Passageways of Memory

In the attic, dust flies high,
Old toys giggle as they sigh.
Pictures dance, shadows play,
Doors creak with tales of the day.

Socks mismatched in the drawer,
Telling secrets, wanting more.
Grandpa's stories sticking like glue,
Such wild trips he claims he flew.

The clock ticks loud with a laugh,
Counting blunders on its path.
Cake crumbs scattered on the floor,
Who forgot to shut the door?

Jars of candy, hidden away,
Making mischief in the fray.
Every sweet holds a jest,
Memory's snack, a joyful quest.

Threads of Temporal Journeys

A sweater knitted long ago,
Stitching gaps of time's own flow.
Purls of laughter, yarns of cheer,
Worn by those who loved us dear.

A rubber band that made a snap,
History caught in a silly trap.
Faded postcards in a stack,
Sending giggles from the past back.

In the quilt, a patch or two,
Whispers from a friend or two.
Stitched-up secrets, tales complete,
Every thread a heartskipped beat.

Napping cats upon the keys,
Chasing shadows, swaying trees.
Weaving time in every doze,
Funny how the world just flows.

Ancestral Footsteps

In the hallway, echoes bounce,
Footsteps of ghosts that like to prounce.
Great Aunt Hilda and her dance,
Every twirl a funny chance.

With slippers worn, she'd glide and sway,
Leaving smiles in her wake each day.
Gramps in slippers too, but loud,
Stories told to an invisible crowd.

Through the garden, weeds take strife,
Grandma's veggies, full of life.
A zucchini that grew so tall,
It holds the record for the fall!

Framed paintings, eyes that wink,
Living tales make you think.
Ancestral antics never fade,
Life's a comedy parade.

Portraits in the Hall of Hours

In the hall, portraits stare,
Laughing at the time we share.
Lady in lace, such a grin,
Caught behind a golden pin.

Mr. Timmy, always late,
His clockwork brain won't cooperate.
Every tick a funny tale,
Time's a boat, but he's off sail.

A dog on the mantle, paws in air,
Did he ever chase a chair?
Lipstick kisses on the frame,
Every face, a quirky claim.

Photos fade, but laughter stays,
Echoing in countless ways.
A gallery of silly sights,
In the hours of joyful nights.

Echoes in the Clock

Tick tock, the clock winks,
With secrets it never thinks.
Each chime a laugh, each tick a tease,
Time's just playing, if you please!

Watch the seconds dance and prance,
In a funny little time-lapse glance.
What was a minute? I can't recall,
Did I forget to feed my pet snail?

Oh, clocks can be such jokers, you see,
Hiding moments behind a cup of tea.
And in the gears, the giggles hide,
As I chase time, trying to abide!

Some days it sprints, some days it crawls,
Rarely shows up when duty calls.
Yet here I am with all my whimsy,
Chasing memories like a busy bee!

Shadows of Forgotten Moments

In the corner, shadows sigh,
Whispering tales of time gone by.
There's the sock I lost somewhere,
And my poor hat left in despair!

The dust bunnies dance, quite absurd,
Each leap accompanied by a word.
"Remember that trip? Oh what a blast!"
Too bad I forgot, it slipped so fast!

Tickling the edges of my mind,
Forgotten jokes are so unkind.
"Ha! Remember when?" echoes awaken,
But my brain's on pause, utterly shaken!

Still, I giggle at what once was,
Making memories without a cause.
And as shadows play their funny game,
I can only laugh, "Ain't that a shame!"

Reflections in a Dusty Mirror

In the glass, my face does grin,
But oh dear, where do I begin?
There's a smudge near my left ear,
Is that a ghost? Or just my beer?

Reflections tease, oh what a sight!
Who knew mirrors could be so spry?
"Remember that hairstyle? All the rage!"
I can't believe I turned that page!

Laughter echoes in the glass,
As old memories come to pass.
"Was that you, dancing like a fool?"
Or just my reflection acting cool?

Yet here I stand, somewhat out of place,
With crusty jokes and a silly face.
In the mirror, I conjure a smile,
For time brings fun when you stay awhile!

The Ticking Pulse of Memory

A heartbeat quick, a laugh or sigh,
Ticking pulses float on by.
What was fun once seems so far,
Like counting sheep, a fuzzy star!

In the rhythm of a silly rhyme,
Each second mocks the flow of time.
Remember the ice cream that flew?
Or the time my shoe stuck to goo?

Memory's clock spins round and round,
In laughter's grip, I'm tightly bound.
Remember when I tripped on air?
Those moments shine, with silly flair!

So let me dance to the ticking tune,
With quirky steps beneath the moon.
For every tick brings joy with glee,
In the silly waltz of memory!

Whispers Carried by the Draft

In corners where the silence creeps,
A sock debates the age of sheep.
The cat gives a conspiratorial glare,
As dust bunnies dance without a care.

The cupboard sighs with tales untold,
Of mismatched socks and spoons of gold.
A dripping tap sings a lazy tune,
As chairs hold court with the light of the moon.

The rug grumbles beneath our feet,
While echoes of laughter taste bittersweet.
A vase subverts its floral role,
Holding secrets in its porcelain soul.

And whispers fly like paper planes,
Carried by drafts with a penchant for games.
In this quirky realm of everyday grunge,
Life's little oddities assemble for fun!

The Scent of Old Photographs

An album with pages like ancient trees,
Holds faces frozen in quirky cheese.
The musty smell of yesteryears,
Makes us laugh, choked over tears.

A cousin's hairdo defies all time,
While uncles pull faces that should be a crime.
With every flip, another surprise,
The fashion faux pas dance before our eyes.

Grandma's spectacles gleam with pride,
Hiding a twinkle she can't quite abide.
In sepia tones, the past hosts a fair,
Revealing the bits we'd rather not share.

But laughter erupts as we take a peek,
At that one cousin who snored like a freak.
With every picture, a memory blooms,
The scent of old tales fills up the rooms.

Shadows Unspooled in the Backroom

In the backroom where shadows play,
Old boxes scheme and hide away.
The broomstick leans like it's had a few,
While shadows entertain a ghost or two.

Old hats dangle from rusty nails,
Whispering secrets of grander tales.
The wallpaper peels with a giggle delight,
As cobwebs weave stories out of sight.

Lost toys stare with button-like eyes,
Plotting mischief, oh what a surprise!
A wooden soldier stands at attention,
Charmed by the dust and its strange dimension.

While shadows gather like old friends,
Their laughter echoes, it never ends.
In this whimsical nook, so tucked away,
Livelihoods thrive in the games they play.

The Lullaby of Clockwork Dreams

Tick tock, the gears all sigh,
As clocks conspire in an endless try.
A pendulum swings with a cheeky blink,
While sleepy eyes begin to sink.

Cogs in rhythm, what a tune!
A lullaby croons to the bright full moon.
When seconds giggle and minutes skip,
The night drifts off on a whimsical trip.

In this world where minutes run,
The clock hands jest, oh what fun!
With winks and nudges, they plot and scheme,
Painting the night with a rubbery dream.

Amidst the clicks, we find our peace,
As whispers of wonder never cease.
With every tick, there's a funny tease,
In the lullaby of dreams that please.

Mists of Yesterday

As I walked past the fridge, so tall,
I swear I heard echoes of a loopy call.
Grandma's meatloaf, from decades past,
Waving goodbye, I thought it wouldn't last.

Pictures hung crooked, the cat on a chair,
Looks like he's plotting some mischief, I swear!
Time flies like dandelions in the breeze,
And I'm just a jester, laughing with ease.

Dust bunnies dance on the floor, they spin,
Each twist and twirl is a chaotic win.
The clock ticks slower, a grand old joke,
I tip my hat to the echoes that poke.

Peeking in closets where remnants reside,
Old shoes and hats, they surely confide.
With laughter and smiles, I shuffle around,
In this funny time warp, I'll never be found.

Historical Reveries

In my dreams, I'm a knight, so noble and bold,
With jelly-filled armor, a sight to behold!
Fighting like pirates, we dine on hot fries,
While turtles debate the best way to fly.

Peering through windows, I see it all clear,
A dance of the past with wobbly cheer.
They argue and giggle, these folks from before,
My grandpa can't find his spare wooden door.

Socks clash with sandals, it's quite the affair,
In this time-warped circus, not a soul seems to care.
Chronicles written with crayon on chalk,
While the rascally cat holds an impromptu talk.

So here in my dreams, I revel and prance,
A historian's coach dance, the world's wild romance.
With giggles and chuckles, let's make history fly,
In a whirlwind of laughter, under a smelly pie!

Gables of the Past

In an old dusty house where the shadows play,
Spiders tell tales of the bread's grand ballet.
A parrot named Roger recites all the news,
While the wallpaper whispers of colorful shoes.

Chairs with the creaks have stories to share,
Of grand tea parties held without a care.
Sandwiches vanished, who knows where they went?
Beneath the old gables, a serious event!

A cat on a ledge with a fanciful air,
Watches the squirrels all gather and stare.
Time's a wild jester, it spins and it flips,
As I laugh with my friends, trading silly quips.

So stroll through these rooms where the past meets today,

In a comedy kingdom, we merrily sway.
With giggles and joy, let nostalgia unwind,
In this merry adventure, the laughter's combined!

Doors that No Longer Open

There's a door that's been locked since way back in '99,
Rumor says treasure—but it's just sticky brine.
I jiggle the handle, it won't budge a bit,
What secrets reside? Oh, do tell me a skit!

Squeaky hinges protest, I give them a shove,
Only to find it's haunted by a glove!
It dances around with an attitude fine,
Throwing a tantrum like some spoiled wine.

Through windows that creak in an oddly-posed way,
A garden of laughter grows day after day.
Old socks and lost toys become heroes tonight,
In a tale where nonsense takes joyous flight.

Behind every door, there's a riddle and jest,
Who knew that old furniture could have such a fest?
With chuckles and giggles, let's try every key,
In a world full of laughter, where wild spirits flee!

The Unraveling of Yesterday

Yesterday wore mismatched socks,
Chasing its tail while cracking jokes.
It spilled coffee on its favorite shirt,
And danced awkwardly with time's quirky quirks.

The clock laughed loud as it ticked away,
While yesterday tried not to sway.
It pulled ribbons from every drawer,
Creating a mess, begging for more.

In the kitchen, it burned toast,
While telling tales of the ghosts that boast.
But every stumble brought a cheer,
For yesterday knew it had no fear.

As the sun peeked in for a prying glance,
Yesterday tripped in a last-minute dance.
With a wink and a grin, it bid adieu,
Promising mischief, as it often would do.

At the Doorway of Dusk

At dusk's threshold, shadows giggle,
Twilight plays a silent wiggle.
With a wink, the stars start to tease,
While crickets dance with graceful ease.

Time's door creaks as laughter spills,
The whisk of wind gives playful chills.
A cat with glasses reads the news,
While streetlamps fight their cozy blues.

The moon in stripes hops on the scene,
Dressed like a jester, all in green.
He tosses jokes with all his might,
As days and nights begin their fight.

With every tick, the colors blend,
While dusk and dawn play pretend.
The silliness of evening's art,
Turns every frown into a spark.

Chronicles of Lost Tomorrows

In the attic, tomorrows stack,
Worn-out chairs and fractal quacks.
They fight for space, a silly brawl,
While yesterday's slippers start to sprawl.

One tomorrow dreams of being bright,
While another likes to sleep at night.
They throw a party, snacks all around,
With jokes and laughter, what a sound!

In the midst of cake, they lose their way,
Forgotten plans for the very next day.
But who needs schedules to have some fun?
The lost tomorrows dance, one by one.

As they swirl through the cluttered space,
Time's foolish smile lights up the place.
With every giggle, futures collide,
In a whirlwind of joy, they take a ride.

In the Nook of Time's Embrace

In a nook where silly moments dwell,
Time's embrace rings like a school bell.
Tick-tock jokes play hide and seek,
While giggles echo, playful and meek.

Dust bunnies debate who's in charge,
As they hop around, they take it large.
A rubber band slingshots across the room,
Creating chaos, and a sense of gloom.

Amidst the clutter, laughter brews,
As time sips tea and shares its views.
With every tick, it makes a prank,
In a swirl of fun, at the time bank.

In that nook, where days collide,
Silliness reigns, and worries hide.
As time unwinds, it grins with glee,
Forty winks with a side of spree.

www.ingramcontent.com/pod-product-compliance
Lightning Source LLC
Chambersburg PA
CBHW060135230426
43661CB00003B/428